Bibliographic information published by the German National Library:

The German National Library lists this publication in the National Bibliography; detailed bibliographic data are available on the Internet at http://dnb.dnb.de .

Imprint:

Copyright © 2018 GRIN Verlag
Print and binding: Books on Demand GmbH, Norderstedt Germany
ISBN: 9783668944992

This book at GRIN:

https://www.grin.com/document/461503

Tanmay Teckchandani

SQL injection attacks and mitigations

Computer application security capstone project

GRIN Verlag

GRIN - Your knowledge has value

Since its foundation in 1998, GRIN has specialized in publishing academic texts by students, college teachers and other academics as e-book and printed book. The website www.grin.com is an ideal platform for presenting term papers, final papers, scientific essays, dissertations and specialist books.

Visit us on the internet:

http://www.grin.com/

http://www.facebook.com/grincom

http://www.twitter.com/grin_com

SQL INJECTION: ATTACKS AND MITIGATIONS

COMPUTER APPLICATION SECURITY CAPSTONE PROJECT
WINTER 2018

FINAL REPORT

Tanmay Teckchandani

Table of contents

INTRODUCTION

Structured Query Language Injection is one of the vulnerabilities in OSWAP Top 10 list for web-based application exploitation. In this study, we will be **demonstrating** the different methods of **SQL injection attacks** and **prevention techniques** will be illustrated.

Web application are widespread as they have become the necessity for the everyday life. Most web-based applications communicate with a database using a machine-understandable language called **Structured Query Language (SQL).**

SQL injection is a code injection technique, used to attack data-driven applications, in which malicious SQL statements are inserted from the client of the application.

PROBLEM STATEMENT

The goal of this study is to spread **awareness** to public out there using internet that what does SQL injection mean, how the websites and web applications can be attacked using SQL injection, why it is one of the greatest security issue in today's world and also how the **developers** should lower the risk of SQL injection Attack when developing the Web Applications.

The main purpose of SQL injection attack is to comprise the database, which is an organized collection of data and supporting data structures. The data can include **sensitive information** like username, passwords, encryptions keys and many organization related information. The main consequences of SQL injection attack are **Confidentiality:** databases have private information which can be a major problem if lost; **Authentication:** using bad SQL commands into application can lead to theft of username and password; **Authorization:** private information like authorization information stored in database; **Integrity:** Altering of information in database [1].

SIGNIFICANCE

SQL injection Attack befalls when an attacker causes the web application to produce SQL queries that are functionally diverse from what user interface programmer intended. The platform affected can be any web application which interacts with a SQL database. **Inadequate input validation, improper programming of SQL statements, laziness while programming applications** can expose the web applications to SQL injection vulnerability. Likelihood of exploit is very high. SQL injection is **number one threat to web application listed by OWASP (Open Web Application Security Project)** and it is a rampant and hypothetically damaging attack [1].

SQL injection is not a new issue. The date of its discovery is ambiguous. However, in last few years. SQL injection Attack have been escalating very fast.

Going 5 years back in 2012, a representative of Barclaycard claimed that 97% of data breaches are a result of SQL injection. The online article states that "In late 2011 through early 2012 i.e. only one month, over one million web pages were affected by the Lilupophilupop SQL injection attack". In 2010, united nations official website was a victim of SQL injection. One can now imagine the greatness of problem of SQL injection.

"The breach of a web server that housed payment card data for a New York tourism company's website highlights security gaps in cardholder data protection". 110,000 credit card information were stolen by hacker using SQL injection in December 2010.

Link: http://www.bankinfosecurity.com/sql-injection-blamed-for-new-breach-a-3195

"The hacktivist group says it obtained the records via SQL injection at government sites". This was reported in 2012 December. 1.6 million accounts at FBI and NASA were exposed.

Link: https://www.cnet.com/news/ghostshell-claims-breach-of-1-6m-accounts-at-fbi-nasa-and-more/

"Hacker group claims to have looted $100k via SQL injection attack". This incident was reported in October 2013.

Link: https://www.scmagazine.com/hacker-group-claims-to-have-looted-100k-via-sql-injection-attack/article/542609/

One of the biggest SQL injection attack, a group of Russian hackers stole more than one billion passwords from sites both big and small. The group used number of internet-connected devices know as botnet to steal the passwords from an estimated 400,000 sites. This was reported in 2014.

Link: https://www.business2community.com/tech-gadgets/russian-hackers-means-website-0979723#!bLWV8O

The year of 2016 faced many SQL injection attacks. In 2016 April, Qatar national bank's database was hacked using SQL injection. It was reported that 1.4GB of data was compromised which had customer information and credit card information.

Link: http://www.ibtimes.co.uk/qatar-national-bank-leak-security-experts-hint-sql-injection-used-database-hack-1557069

In may 2016, hacker used SQL injection to get inside the Drupal sites and installed fake ransomware.

The first victims recorded complaining about this new strain of ransomware appeared in late March, on the official Drupal forums. Site admins were describing their websites as "being locked" with a message that read:

" Website is locked. Please transfer 1.4 BitCoin to address 3M6SQh8Q6d2j1B4JRCe2ESRLHT4vTDbSM9 to unlock content. "

Link: http://news.softpedia.com/news/crooks-used-sql-injections-to-hack-drupal-sites-and-install-web-ransomware-504300.shtml

The DotA 2 forum was hacked in July 2016 and user's personal information were leaked such as ip addresses, passwords. The gaming forum was hacked and 1,972,972 records were exposed.

Link: https://www.digitaltrends.com/computing/dota2-forum-hacked-two-mollion-sql-injection/

"Attackers used a flaw in the internet forum software vBulletin to breach 11 websites, exposing 27 Million accounts". It is a huge number and was hacked using SQL injection in August 2016.

Link: https://www.scmagazine.com/hackers-exploit-vbulletin-flaw-to-access-27m-accounts-on-11-websites/article/530194/

As of February 2017, the hacker named Rasputin breaches over 60 Universities and government agencies. The online article states that hacker developed his own SQL injection scanner and used it to find weak points and take over vulnerable targets. The hacker then sold leaked information to criminal underground.

Link: https://www.bleepingcomputer.com/news/security/hacker-rasputin-breaches-over-60-universities-and-government-agencies/

In October 2017, few months back 130k accounts were affected at Arden Hills-based catholic financial service provider. The forensic investigation determined that the company's web server had been attacked via SQL injection.

Link: https://www.twincities.com/2017/10/16/catholic-united-financial-data-breach-may-have-affected-nearly-130k-accounts/

The online article posted online in August 2017 says that SQL injection is still a leading method of CYBER ATTACK.

Link: https://www.alertlogic.com/blog/tried-and-true-sql-injection-still-a-leading-method-of-cyber-attack/

RESOURCES

We will be using C# ASP.NET technology along with MS SQL Server database to demonstrate the SQL Injection Attacks and Countermeasures.

We have opted for the above technology because most of the organizations use those technology and Microsoft SQL Database is used widely around in world by most of the organizations and developers. MSSQL has many features that most of the organizations requires for developing Web Applications according to user standards.

SUMMARY: WEB SEARCH AND LITERATURE

This section is focused on summarizing the above web search, few literatures and recent rending reports on SQL injection. The above web articles on SQL injection attacks i.e. from December 2010 to August 2017 conclude that concern for SQL injection evolved year by year. The above articles suggest, most of the organizations suffered biggest loss of financial information. Popular government agencies FBI and NASA were the victim of SQL injection attack, were 1.6 million accounts were compromised. The group called hacktivist said it stole records using SQL injection at government sites and posted the records online. Hackers use different [7] attack patterns to get inside the databases of web application. Patterns can include using combinations of various attacks, using variety of tools for SQL injection such as SQL map and different approaches using SQL injection queries. The article from May 2016 states that hacker used SQL injection attack to get inside and then installed ransomware malware to encrypt the information.

The literatures state, the major impacts of SQL injection are data leak or loss, authentication bypass, denial of access, destruction of database or information. These major impacts were faced by most of the companies which were hacked via SQL injection. Article from October 2017 states financial company's web server was hacked using SQL injection were 130k members accounts got compromised. Further, the financial company removed all potential access to personally identifiable records on their server and secured the web server from any possible further attack. This was the recent incident which occurred last year i.e. 2017 on 6th September.

Online article dated 30th June 2017 says that WordPress plugin which is used by 300,00+ websites is vulnerable to SQL injection attack [8]. "WordPress plugin WP statistics is vulnerable to SQL injection flaw that allows a remote attacker, with at least a subscriber account, to steal sensitive information from the website's database and possibly gain unauthorized access to websites". From the statement we can conclude that SQL injection is evolving very fast. Another article from May 2017 states that UK based Information Commissioner's Office fined Euro 55,000 to an e-commerce firm as their website was vulnerable to SQL injection [9]. Information Security firms are straightway penalizing organizations because of not securing their websites. One can now imagine how the huge the concern of SQL injection is. Finally, an article dated 7th November 2016 says that researchers found SQL injection vulnerability in IOT device, in which an attacker can inject malicious SQL code into paired IOT device's mobile application and take root control of IOT device [10].

METHODOLOGY

Most of the web search in significance section shows that web applications were attacked by performing SQL injection from their login panel or a panel which has to do with user input. The organization who were the victim of SQL injection suffered huge amount of data breach and some organizations data were dumped and some companies suffered huge financial loss. We are doing research on this topic to spread awareness among web developers and people with less knowledge of SQL injection. So, that web application with databases which contains confidential data can be prevented in coming future. As, data is the most crucial asset to protect.

Databases are the main target for hackers because database contains sensitive information. Therefore, databases are often targeted for acquiring sensitive information by performing SQL injection attack which is listed number one in OWASP top ten list of web application security risk. This section is focused upon which methods we will use to demonstrate SQL injection attack and different approaches for mitigating SQL injection vulnerability.

We will be developing one simple website which will has username and password as textbox, one login button and sign up button. When user logs in to website using credentials he/she will be redirected to welcome page with some user details. When a new user wants to sign up he/she will sign up and information of that user will be stored in database. This website will be vulnerable to SQL injection attack and we will show how this web-site can be attacked using SQL injection to gain access to any user's account, deleting tables in database, inserting records, showing application errors from which information about database can be obtained. Then, we will develop **three** web-sites which has same design as described above but each web-site will have different approach to mitigate SQL injection vulnerability.

For mitigating SQL injection vulnerability three different methods will be demonstrated. First method will be using **parameterized query** also known as prepared statements. Parameterized query is the first approach developers should be taught when writing database queries. Moreover, parameterized queries force developers to first define all SQL code, then pass in each parameter to query later. This coding style allows database to distinguish between code and data, regardless of what user input is supplied [11]. Another approach we will be using is **stored procedures**. Stored procedures will be created in database, which will perform the query and query will be parameterized query. So, it will be the combination of stored procedure and parameterized query. As stored procedures are defined in database itself it will be then called from an application rather than something

6

that user is allowed to enter. Last approach will be demonstrating is **input validation**. Input validation is used to detect unauthorized input before it is processed by an application which results in preventing SQL injection attack. We will be validating user input by checking its type, length, format and range. Additionally, we will be showing custom error pages instead of showing database error information to user. Custom error pages will have some limited error detail to client screen. So, the client has less information which he/she cannot use to obtained database information, thereby preventing SQL injection attack.

Furthermore, we would like to talk about difference between proposed methods. Stored procedures are not always safe from SQL injection. The difference between parameterized query and stored procedures is that SQL code for stored procedure is defined and stored in database itself and called from an application [11] while in parameterized query SQL statements are written in code with variable binding. Therefore, both approaches have same effectiveness in preventing SQL injection.

For developing websites, we will be using specific tools and technology. We will be developing SQL injection vulnerable website plus three different methods for mitigating SQL injection vulnerability with **Microsoft Visual studio 2017** alongside backend database server will be **Microsoft SQL server 2017**. In visual studio 2017, we will be developing ASP.NET website with simple login panel, sign up panel and user welcome page. All the websites will be developed in C# language in Microsoft Visual Studio 2017 and websites will be connected to backend database server which is Microsoft SQL server 2017. SQL is widely used database language and Microsoft SQL server is used by most of the organization in today's world.

Finally, we would say that information gathered from web search helped us in proposing the different methods to mitigate SQL injection vulnerability. Proposed methods will be helpful to anyone going through this document and they will have clear understanding of SQL injection and their prevention methods.

RESULTS AND DISCUSSION

In this section we will be demonstrating results of work on the proposed methods described in previous chapter. Also, this section includes what challenges we faced while developing the proposed methods.

Vulnerable website: We have developed a simple website which is vulnerable to **SQL INJECTION.** Here, we have demonstrated different types SQL injection attack i.e. which can delete database and records from database, retrieve records of database, show errors where application code is visible and insert values into database by performing SQL injection attack on this website. This website is built with simple GUI with login form, registration form and welcome page where it shows user is logged in. Below is the basic look and feel of a website and we have developed same GUI for all the three solutions.

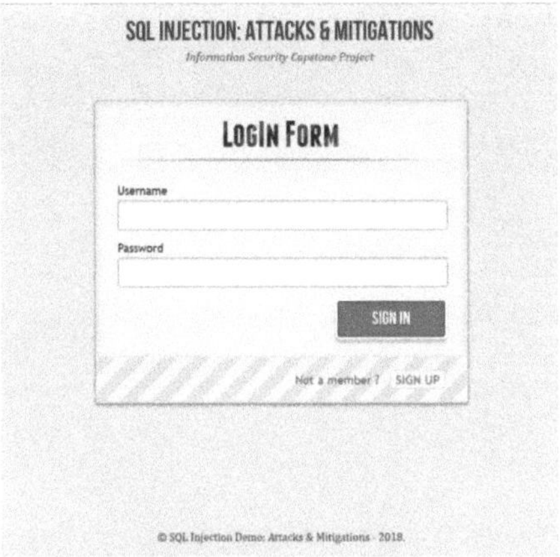

SQL INJECTION: ATTACKS & MITIGATIONS

Information Security Capstone Project

LOGIN FORM

Username

Password

SIGN IN

Not a member ? SIGN UP

© SQL Injection Demo: Attacks & Mitigations - 2018.

SQL INJECTION: ATTACKS & MITIGATIONS

Information Security Capstone Project

REGISTRATION FORM

Username

Email ID

Password

Confirm Password

CREATE ACCOUNT

Already a member ? SIGN IN

© SQL Injection Demo: Attacks & Mitigations - 2018.

Performed SQL Injection Attacks on vulnerable website

1. Inserting values into database from login form. Second screen capture shows the data is
   added in table in backend database view.

9

[Image has been removed by the editorial staff due to privacy reasons.]

2. Error message which shows the application code

SQL INJECTION: ATTACKS & MITIGATIONS
Information Security Capstone Project

LOGIN FORM

Username

` ' having 1=1-|`

Password

SIGN IN

Not a member ? SIGN UP

Column 'Registration.us ×

← → C ① localhost:63151/Login.aspx

Server Error in '/' Application.

Column 'Registration.username' is invalid in the select list because it is not contained in e

Description: An unhandled exception occurred during the execution of the current web request. Please review the stack trace for more information about the error and

Exception Details: System.Data.SqlClient.SqlException: Column 'Registration.username' is invalid in the select list because it is not contained in either an aggregate

Source Error:

```
Line 23:             connection.Open();
Line 24:             SqlCommand command = new SqlCommand(sqlcmd, connection);
Line 25:             SqlDataReader reader = command.ExecuteReader();
Line 26:             if (reader.Read())
Line 27:             {
```

Source File: D:\Computer Security - Conestoga\Winter_2018\Security Project\Practical Solution\CapstoneProject\CapstoneProject\CapProj_vulnerable\Login.aspx.cs

10

3. Deleting table from database. This query can destroy the table and delete all the records from table. Firstly, one can see the table named registration in below screen capture, as soon as SQL query for dropping table is injected into username field and press sign in button, it deletes the table from database.

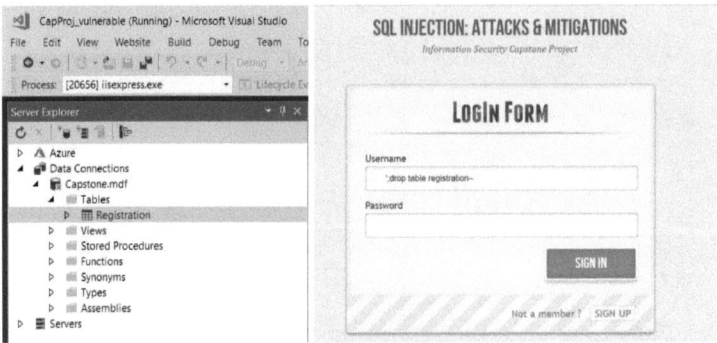

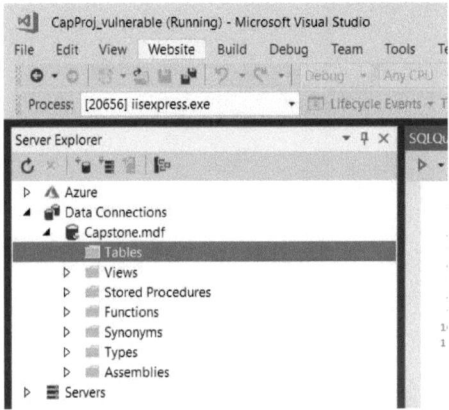

4. Lastly, SQL query injected in username field to login if username is known without entering the password. Second screen capture shows user is logged in.

For mitigating SQL injection vulnerability in this website, we have developed three solutions were an attacker cannot perform the above demonstrated SQL injection attacks.

First Solution: Parameterized Query is the one of the solution to mitigate SQL injection vulnerability. It is also known as prepared statement. It is a type of SQL query that requires at least one parameter for execution. A placeholder is normally substituted for the parameter in SQL query. The parameter is then passed to the query in a separate statement [13].

When developing this solution, we had to do some research on how to implement this solution in application development and how to write the backend code and how it works on .Net framework. We successfully implemented this solution without facing any problems as we had some knowledge of it and rest we researched on internet and implemented it.

The code behind is implemented where we have created two objects of sqlparameter respectively for username and password where we take input from user and store into created sqlparameter objects. User inputted data is then checked by database and if username and password are correct and matches the values in database, user is shown with their login screen.

```
SqlParameter usernameparameter = new SqlParameter("@username", SqlDbType.NVarChar, 25) { Value = this.username.Text };
command.Parameters.Add(usernameparameter);
SqlParameter passwordparameter = new SqlParameter("@password", SqlDbType.NVarChar, 25) { Value = this.password.Text };
command.Parameters.Add(passwordparameter);
```

After implementing this solution, we tested it and we found that it worked successfully. Below is the screen capture where attacker cannot perform SQL injection attack on website.

Here, as soon as the attacker tries to login with this query the page is redirected to a custom error page. We have also created custom error page for all the three solutions where an error message is shown instead of error generated by application itself.

Strengths of this solution is that it avoids common SQL injection because database is forced to interpret everything that comes within the bound variables as data and not as SQL queries. One of the weakness of this solution is that since queries are written in application code, one could end with same query in multiple places.

We have tested this solution on web browsers that includes IE, Firefox, chrome, edge. This solution is compatible to web browser mentioned.

Second Solution: Stored Procedure is another way to prevent web-based application from SQL injection attacks. It is a set of SQL statements which are stored in database itself as a group and a name is assigned to it. One of the advantage of using stored procedure is, it can be reused and shared with multiple programs. We have used stored procedure as it is very important from Web Application Security perspective. Stored procedure provides an important layer of security between user interface and the database. As stored procedures are written in database so, the user cannot see or change it. A stored procedure preserves data integrity because information is entered in a consistent manner as it improves productivity because statements in a stored procedure must be written only once.

Here, we have created stored procedure named "GetLogin" with prepared statement in database itself. Then, we are using "GetLogin" in program logic with created sqlparameter objects.

```
CREATE PROCEDURE dbo.GetLogin

    @username nvarchar(25),
    @password nvarchar(25)

AS
SELECT * FROM Registration WHERE username=@username AND password=@password
```

```
connection.Open();
string sqlCommand = "GetLogin";
SqlCommand cmd = new SqlCommand(sqlCommand, connection);
cmd.CommandType = CommandType.StoredProcedure;
SqlParameter p1 = new SqlParameter("@username", SqlDbType.NVarChar, 25)
{
    Value = username.Text
};
cmd.Parameters.Add(p1);
SqlParameter p2 = new SqlParameter("@password", SqlDbType.NVarChar, 25)
{
    Value = password.Text
};
cmd.Parameters.Add(p2);
```

When developing this solution, we faced some challenges that how to use the created stored procedure in application logic while creating stored procedure in database was an easy part. At last, we successfully implemented this solution with some research on how to use stored procedure in application code.

After implementing solution, we performed some SQL injection attacks to test if we can break in and we found that solution worked perfectly and did not affect the database. Below is one of the test result of failed SQL injection attack.

When trying to injection drop table query, it fails and in database the table is not deleted and records are also not deleted.

One of the advantage of using this solution all logic related to client-database interaction is stored in one place and user cannot see it in application logic as it is stored in SQL server database. Weakness of implementing this solution is a Database Admin is required for performance tuning and thus cost is increased. Also, extra load on database.

This is solution is also tested on web browser that includes IE, Firefox, chrome, edge and works perfectly with no performance difference and compatible with browser mentioned above.

Third Solution: **Input Validation** is another nice way to prevent web applications from SQL injection attacks. When user inputs username and password the validator checks if the username and password are valid or not.

When developing this solution, we had to research about how to implement regular expression validator in asp.net and also how not to include characters such semi-colon, dashes and apostrophe. After research, we implemented those controls on our web-site and we were successful in implementing validation controls. The website works smoothly with validation controls.

Here, we have used validation controls provided by asp.net which is known as asp.net validator controls. Validation controls such as regular expression validator and required field validator have been used in this solution. This validator controls the input given by user in textbox and if the user input is incorrect the validator control shows appropriate error message to user and user cannot sign in to their account until they provide correct credentials.

To prevent SQL injection attacks, we have used regular expression where user cannot use apostrophe ('), semicolons (;), dashes (-). User can only use alphabets i.e. lower and upper case and numbers in username field and if user inputs no data into username field it shows error message "Username is required" i.e. use of required field validator. Below screen capture shows how we have used required field validator and regular expression validator controls. Also, we have implemented these controls on registration page when user creates an account.

ControlToValidate="username" ErrorMessage="USERNAME IS REQUIRED!" ForeColor="Red"></asp:RequiredFieldValidator>

"server" ControlToValidate="username" ErrorMessage="NOT VALID USERNAME!" ValidationExpression="^[a-zA-Z0-9\s]{1,15}$" ForeColor="Red"></asp:Reg

Now, the demonstration of required field validator and regular expression validator is shown in below screen captures.

When user try to enter semi-colon in username field and it shows an appropriate error message to user. Below is the screen capture.

Advantage of implementing this solution is it validates user on client-side before communicating with database and developer can write custom validations according to organization needs and restricting user for not using characters like dashes, semi-colon, apostrophe which can harm database. One of the disadvantage is user would be restricted for using only limited characters, which will result in less secure credentials.

Lastly, we have tested this solution on web browser that includes IE, Firefox, chrome, edge and we found that there is no to little difference when running this solution on web browser mentioned above and therefore is compatible to browsers mentioned above.

Finally, we would say that we have successfully implemented all the proposed methods. Also, we faced some challenges while implementing those controls, that are mentioned in each solution's section.

CONCLUSION AND RECOMMENDATIONS

The paper discusses different SQL injection attacks and prevention techniques which has been proposed in above chapter. We first define SQL injection vulnerability in web application, then demonstrate different threats to SQL injection vulnerability and lastly present three different solutions to mitigate SQL injection vulnerability.

The three different prevention techniques to prevent SQL injection attack which we proposed are parameterized query, stored procedure and input validation. The only difference between stored procedure and parameterized query is stored procedures are stored at database level and parameterized query is a query that accepts parameters from the DML (Data Manipulation Language) statement in application logic. There is no difference in respect to performance or security (almost) i.e. both methods can equally protect web applications from SQL injection attacks. But there is a big difference in both approaches when in different situations. So, parameterized queries are excellent for projects that have a single application and modest security requirements i.e. applications using single web-page which communicates with database and that database is used only for that application and on other hand, if database is handled by multiple applications and need to enforce consistency of access or need complex security (partial access to tables, either by column or row or both) then one should use stored procedures. Also, stored procedure allows developers to enforce security requirements and provide consistent interface so applications don't violate data rules. Furthermore, input validation validates user-supplied data and developers can user custom validation according to client needs. Importantly, the huge difference between input validation and other two solutions (stored procedure and parameterized query) i.e. inputs by user is validated at client-side before any communication with database while stored procedure and parameterized query checks user inputted data with the data stored in database and then grants user access. Therefore, input validation can be used in web application to prevent SQL injection attacks as it limits special characters (dashes, semi-colon and apostrophe) used in SQL injection attacks.

For all the negative impact of SQL injection vulnerability, the proposed countermeasures are surprisingly simple to enact. We believe that proposed mitigation techniques cannot provide complete safety against SQL injection attacks, but a combination or mixed approach from presented solutions will cover wide range of SQL injection attacks which will result in a more secure and reliable database against SQL injection attacks. We recommend the use of mixed approach of stored procedure and input validation in order to mitigate threats related to SQL injection vulnerability in a web application. We recommend this mixed approach because combination of stored procedures and input validation makes security of database stronger as stored procedures are generally more efficient since the database can optimize them and store the execution plan also, keeps the data logic close to data, and the business logic out of database and input validation validates user-supplied data before communicating with database and if user input is not valid, user cannot access the application.

In the end, the proposed model is ideal for web application developers in order to protect against SQL injection attacks in the web application. The practical result shows that the proposed model can defend wide range of SQL injection attacks.

SUMMARY

This section summarizes the proposed Information Security Capstone Project on SQL injection Attacks and Mitigations.

Open Web Application Security Project (OWASP) which focuses on improving security of software, has listed SQL (Structured Query Language) injection a top most vulnerability. The journey of static to dynamic web pages leads to the use of database in web applications. Because of lack of secure coding techniques, SQL injection wins in a large set of web applications. A successful SQL injection attack exploits a security vulnerability occurring in database layer of a web application and a service.

This article provides taxonomy on SQL injection Attacks and Prevention methods. Firstly, we provide the purpose of choosing the topic (SQL injection) and why the problem still exists in web applications. Then, we researched and provide bunch of online articles on SQL injection attacks that includes huge data breaches happened because of SQL injection attacks. In addition, we mentioned the amount of data loss due to SQL injection attacks from research articles and propose tools that we used for demonstrating SQL injection attacks and mitigation techniques. Furthermore, we provide description and practical demonstration on how SQL injection attack is performed on web applications and three prevention methods on securing web applications from SQL injection attack. Also, we provide strengths and weaknesses of proposed three solutions, then compare those solutions with each other. Finally, we recommend the best solution for securing web applications from SQL injection attack. In the end, we conclude that proposed model proves to be efficient in the context of its ability to prevent wide-range of SQL injection attacks.

REFERENCES

1. https://www.pinterest.de/pin/353180795770388472/
2. https://www.owasp.org/index.php/SQL_Injection
3. http://cwe.mitre.org/data/definitions/89.html
4. http://www.zdnet.com/article/sql-injection-attack-what-is-it-and-how-to-prevent-it/
5. https://www.cisco.com/c/en/us/about/security-center/sql-injection.html
6. https://www.netsparker.com/blog/web-security/sql-injection-vulnerability-history/
7. https://www.htbridge.com/vulnerability/sql-injection.html
8. https://thehackernews.com/2017/06/wordpress-hacking-sql-injection.html
9. https://www.infosecurity-magazine.com/news/ico-fines-e-commerce-firm-after/
10. https://www.csoonline.com/article/3138935/security/sqli-xss-zero-days-expose-belkin-iot-devices-android-smartphones.html
11. https://www.owasp.org/index.php/SQL_Injection_Prevention_Cheat_Sheet
12. https://www.rapid7.com/fundamentals/sql-injection-attacks/
13. https://www.techopedia.com/definition/24414/parameterized-query